UH-1 Huey

Written by David Doyle

In Action®

7929

Squadron Signal Publications

Illustrations by Vincenzo Auletta

(Front Cover) UH-1Ds prepare to airlift elements of the 2nd Battalion, 14th Infantry Regiment, from the Filhol Rubber Plantation to a new staging area during Operation Wahiawa near Củ Chi in the Republic of Vietnam on 16 May 1966. (National Archives)

(Back Cover) A UH-1Y Venom assigned to Marine Aviation Weapons and Tactics Squadron One (MAWTS-1) prepares to engage targets during an offensive air-support exercise at Chocolate Mountain Aerial Gunnery Range in California on 28 September 2016. More than 50 years after the initial flight of the Huey, the type remains in service with militaries around the world including the United States Marine Corps. (DVIDS)

About the In Action® Series

In Action® books, despite the title of the genre, are books that trace the development of a single type of aircraft, armored vehicle, or ship from prototype to the final production variant. Experimental or "one-off" variants can also be included. Our first In Action® book was printed in 1971.

ISBN 978-0-89747-843-4

Military/Combat Photographs and Snapshots

If you have any photos of aircraft, armor, soldiers, or ships of any nation, particularly wartime snapshots, please share them with us and help make Squadron/Signal's books all the more interesting and complete in the future. Any photograph sent to us will be copied and returned as requested. Electronic images are preferred. The donor will be fully credited for any photos used. Please send them to:

Squadron/Signal Publications
1115 Crowley Drive
Carrollton, TX 75006-1312 U.S.A.
www.Squadron.com

(Title Page) The U.S. Air Force 20th Special Operations Squadron "Green Hornets" fly UH-1Ps on a sortie in Vietnam. UH-1P 65-7929, foreground, and UH-1P 63-13162 both carry a pair of Miniguns. Each Minigun can unleash a hail of 4,000 7.62mm rounds per minute per gun. On the helicopter in the foreground the Miniguns are augmented by a pair of seven-tube 2.75 rocket launchers. (Capt. Billie Dee Tedford via National Museum of the United States Air Force)

Acknowledgments

This book was completed with the considerable help of my friends Tom Kailbourn, Jim Gilmore, Dana Bell, Sean Hert, Bob Steinbrunn and Scott Taylor. The resources of the National Archives, Army Aviation Museum, National Museum of Naval Aviation, the San Diego Air and Space Museum, Brett Stolle at the National Museum of the United States Air Force, Geoff Cottrell, Paul Hamblin, U.S. Army, and Squadron/Signal Publications (SSP) provided many of the images. This book, nor any of the others, could have been completed without the ongoing help and support of my darling wife Denise.

Introduction

Officially known as the Iroquois, in keeping with U.S. Army policy to name helicopters after Native American nations, the UH-1 is more commonly known as the Huey. The XH-40 prototype first flew in 1956. The aircraft was intended to be a medical evacuation and utility helicopter to replace the Bell H-13 Sioux from the Korean War.

The aircraft was developed by Bell Helicopter and was revolutionary by being powered by a turboshaft engine. When the Army awarded the initial production contract in March 1960, the helicopter was designated the HU-1A – from which designation the name "Huey" was derived. In September 1962 it was redesignated as the UH-1 in accordance with the unified Department of Defense designation system, but the name Huey stuck.

Thanks in a large part to media coverage, the Huey became as much of a symbol of U.S. GI presence in Vietnam as the jeep had been during WWII. From delivery of troops into the field to evacuation of wounded the UH-1 was linked to the public perception of the war. Even when CIA personnel evacuated their apartment during the fall of Saigon, an Air America Huey made the extraction.

In addition to its service before the U.S. involvement in Vietnam, the Huey served long afterward. The sight and sound of the Huey as it passed overhead was familiar to U.S. service men in every conflict through the remainder of the 20th century and into the 21st century as well. In fact, the U.S. Marines UH-1Y "Venom" first deployed in 2009 and was in production until 2016. The UH-1Y is expected to remain part of the force into the 2030s.

An early step in the Huey construction was this wooden scale model attached to a tripod on 29 September 1954. Bell Helicopter Division developed the new utility helicopter to meet Army requirements in 1954. The rotary-wing aircraft was called the XH-40. (Army Aviation Museum)

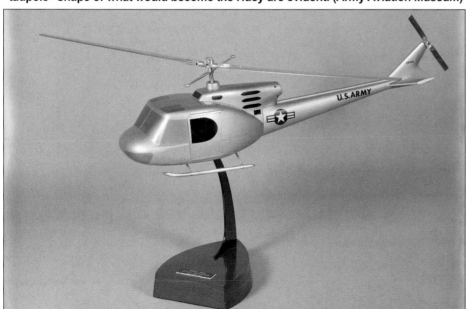

A scale model of Bell's Model 204 utility helicopter is displayed on 13 October 1954. Bell developed the helicopter in the mid-1950s for utility and medical evacuation use. Model 204 was the internal Bell company designation for the aircraft. The general lines and "tadpole" shape of what would become the Huey are evident. (Army Aviation Museum)

Before work began on operable prototypes of the Bell Model 204, this full-scale mockup was constructed. The stencil aft of the sliding door identifies it as "XH-40." The rotor blades are not installed, but the stabilizer bars are present, halfway up the rotor mast. (Army Aviation Museum)

3

A technician works in front of the instrument panel on an XH-40 prototype under construction on 6 August 1956. The Army awarded Bell a contract to build three XH-40 prototypes in June 1955. (Army Aviation Museum)

Power for the XH-40 prototypes was provided by a Lycoming XT53-L-1 gas turbine engine rated at 700 shaft horsepower. Gas turbine engines had several advantages over piston engines. The advantages include lighter weight, smaller size, ease of maintenance, and far more power per engine pound. (Army Aviation Museum)

The left side of a Bell XH-40 helicopter features access to Lycoming XT53-L-1 gas-turbine engine. The engine produced power, which drove a shaft that ran forward to the rotor transmission. After multi-fuel combustion, gases emit through an exhaust nozzle located at the rear of the assembly. (Army Aviation Museum)

Workers construct the first XH-40 at Bell Helicopter's Hurst plant in Texas on 6 August 1956. Paper protects the windows above the nose. The Lycoming engine is installed behind the cabin and above the tail boom. (Army Aviation Museum)

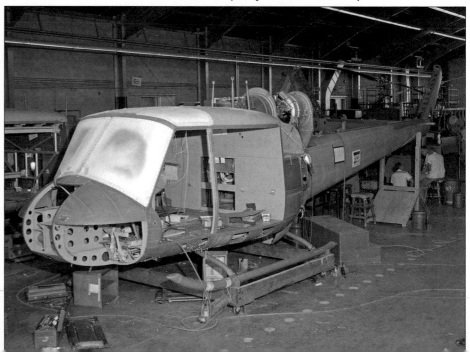

A completed XH-40 prototype is ready to fly. The prototype lead to the long-lasting Bell UH-1 family of helicopters. The three XH-40s marked the start of a new generation of utility helicopters that would be tougher, faster and more versatile than their Korean War counterparts. The Army wanted a helicopter that could carry an 800-pound payload 100 nautical miles at a speed of 100 knots, and could execute a hover up to 6,000 feet. The XH-40 and its successors met and surpassed these goals. (Army Aviation Museum)

Specifications

	UH-1B	UH-1D	UH-1N	UH-1Y
Engine make	Lycoming	Lycoming	Pratt & Whitney	GE
Engine model	T53-L-11	T53-L-11	PTCT-3	T700-GE-401C
Horsepower	1,100	1,100	1,100 x 2	1,800 x 2
Rotor diameter	44 ft	48 ft	48 ft 2¼-inches	48 ft 10 inches
Length overall	53 ft	57 ft 1 inches	57 ft 3¼-inches	58 ft 4 inches
Fuselage length	38 ft 5 inches	41 ft 6 inches	42 ft 4¾-inches	48 ft 9 inches
Height overall	14 ft 7 inches	14 ft 5 inches	14 ft 5 inches	14 ft 7 inches
Empty weight	4,502 lbs	4,920 lbs	6,100 lbs	11,840 lbs
Loaded weight	9,500 lbs	9,500 lbs	10,500 lbs	18,500 lbs
Cruising speed	138 mph	125 mph	126 mph	158 mph
Service ceiling	21,000 ft	19,390 ft	17,300 ft	20,000 ft
Hover ceiling	8,200 ft		12,900 ft	
Range	286 miles	315 miles	248 miles	260 miles

A Bell XH-40 prototype hovers at a low level. Its engine fairing and the cabin doors are not installed. The leading edge of the tail and the spine fairing were left off and exposed the drive shafts for engineers. The Bell XH-40 first flew on 22 October 1956. (Army Aviation Museum)

The first Bell prototype, XH-40 55-4459, conducts an early test flight. Although some sources state that the first XH-40 had no stabilizer bar, one is clearly present below the rotor blades on the main shaft. The XH-40s had a dome-shaped transmission fairing. (Army Aviation Museum)

The second XH-40 prototype performs a test flight over Texas. It has a rotor bar below the rotor blades. An arc-shaped, annular-combustion engine air intake is incorporated into the fairing between the transmission and the engine. A pod with test equipment is above the rotor hub. A large No. 2 is marked on the tail pylon. (Army Aviation Museum)

The third prototype, XH-40 55-4461, makes its first flight from Bell Helicopter's Hurst plant in Texas on 20 November 1957. The third prototype was noteworthy in that the rotor stabilizer was positioned on the main shaft above the rotor blades rather than under the blades as it was on the second XH-40 – and as modified on the first XH40. The rotor stabilizer (stabilizer bar) produces inertia and gyroscopic action that is translated into the rotor system to improve stability in all flight conditions. (Army Aviation Museum)

Bell XH-40 prototype No. 3 performs a low hover. The dark spot on the belly aft of the national insignia is where the cargo hook would be installed. The two dark-colored, horizontal posts on the nose hold radio homing antennas. (Army Aviation Museum)

Engineers work on the third XH-40. Counterweights dangle from the rotor-blade attachment points near the rotor hub. Louvered vents are near the bottom of the sliding door while horizontal louvers are on the lower rear of the cabin. (Army Aviation Museum)

Bell employees work on XH-40 prototype No. 3. The rotor blades each feature a single extruded spar fabricated from a light alloy. The stabilizer bar above the main rotor blades was patented by Bell Helicopter. On the rear of the tail boom was a tail "stinger" skid to protect the boom from damage and keep the tail rotor out of the dirt during nose-high landings. On this pilot, the arc-shaped air scoop was omitted between the transmission and engine fairings. (Army Aviation Museum)

A YH-40 service-test helicopter rests on its skids near a hangar. Before the first XH-40 prototype's initial flight, the Army ordered six YH-40 service-test helicopters from Bell. These were powered by Lycoming T53-L-1A gas-turbine engines, which were rated at 770 shaft horsepower. The cabin was extended 12 inches more than the XH-40. It had capacity for six passengers or two stretchers and a medic. Both the Army and the Air Force tested YH-40s during 1957. A lower fairing with a large frontal air inlet replaced the dome-shaped fairing on XH-40s. Counterweights are located under the rotor hub. The stabilizer bar is above the rotor blades. The bow-shaped annular combustion engine air intake is between the transmission and engine fairings. It retained the lightening holes of various sizes in the bulkhead near the chin window. (Army Aviation Museum)

YH-40 56-6723, the first Bell YH variant, rests on its skids near a hangar. The helicopter was finished overall in an aluminum lacquer or dope. Detachable wheels to handle the helicopter on the ground were mounted on the landing skids. (Army Aviation Museum)

A pilot flies a Bell YH-40 during a test around 1957. The cockpit roof features large windows. On the inboard sides of these windows are air scoops for ventilation. Above the rear of the engine fairing is an anti-collision light. (Army Aviation Museum)

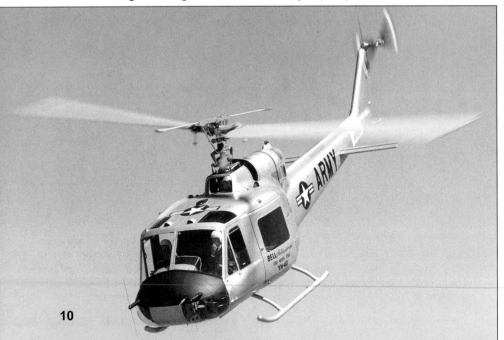

A mechanic works on the turbine engine while the man on the ground adjusts a component inside the cabin section. Ground and air crewmen liked how access panels latched and unlatched with ease on the YH-40 and subsequent UH-1 models. Interior Green paint is visible on the cabin interior and the insides of the access doors. (Bell)

YH-40 56-6726, the fourth in the series, performs a low-level flight over Texas on 10 July 1958. A yellow band with a warning message to keep away from the tail rotor was a standard feature on the tail booms. (Army Aviation Museum)

YH-40 56-6724, the second in the series, hovers low over the Bell Helicopter heliport during a test flight on 2 May 1958 in Hurst, Texas. The Army assigned serial numbers 56-6723 to 66-6728 to the six YH-40s. (Army Aviation Museum)

U.S. Army Transportation Research Command had Bell modify YH-40-BF 56-6723 to the Model 533 to research rotor systems and drag reduction in 1959. Changes included a cambered vertical tail and a new variable-tilt rotor mast. (Army Aviation Museum)

UH-1 Huey Development

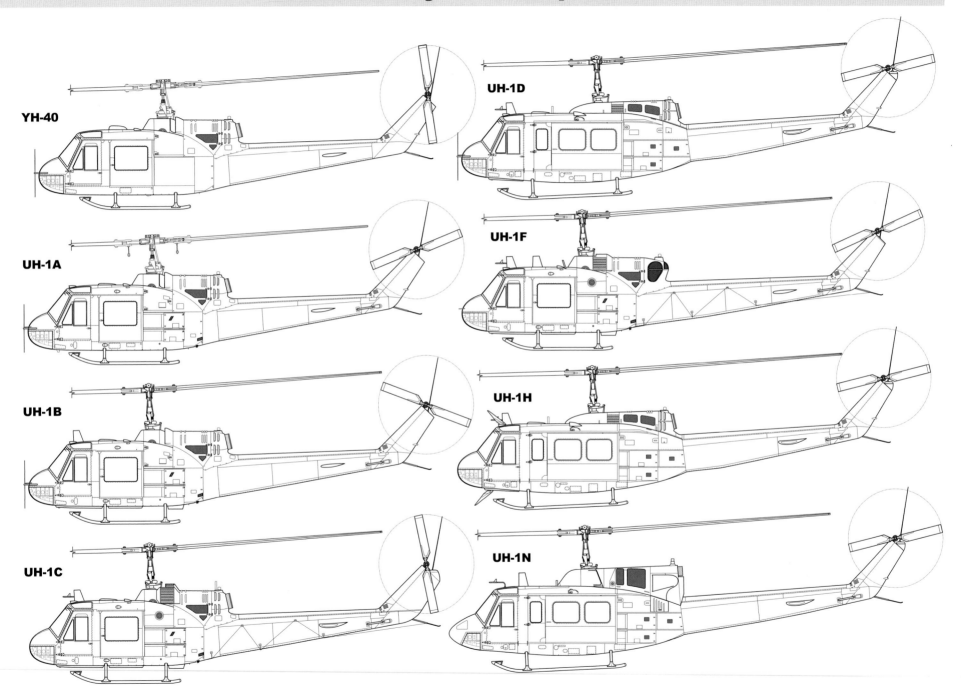

YH-40

UH-1A

UH-1B

UH-1C

UH-1D

UH-1F

UH-1H

UH-1N

HU-1A 58-3017 lands at Shell Army Heliport in Fort Rucker, Alabama. It was one of a several HU-1As converted into trainers with high-visibility orange trim. The first production model to follow the XH-40 prototypes and YH-40 service-test helicopters was the HU-1A. Formally named the Iroquois, the Huey nickname stuck because it was a play on the "HU" prefix of its designation. Bell delivered the first example to the Army on 30 June 1959 – the same month the HU-1A first flew. The HU-1As were initially powered by the Lycoming T53-L-1A turbine engine. Later, the T53-L-5 engine was used. The HU-1A was redesignated the UH-1A under the terms of the tri-service uniform aircraft designation system in September 1962. (National Archives)

HU-1A 59-1693 was outfitted as a trainer with bright orange sections painted over the base coat of Olive Drab. A total of 14 of the initial HU-1 production order were converted to trainers with dual controls and blind-flying instruments. (Army Aviation Museum)

An HU-1A trainer is armed with the M22 Armament Subsystem, which constitutes three AGM-22 missiles on launch racks on each side of the cabin. The AGM-22 was a wire-guided antitank missile based on the French SS.11 missile. (Army Aviation Museum)

The HU-1A/UH-1A had a shorter rotor mast than the HU-1B/UH-1B. The HU-1A/UH-1A had counterweights below the rotor blades, while the counterweights of the HU-1B/UH-1B were above the rotors. Additionally, the HU-1A fuselage was 2 feet, 7 inches shorter than the HU-1B.

Rotor Masts

Fuselage

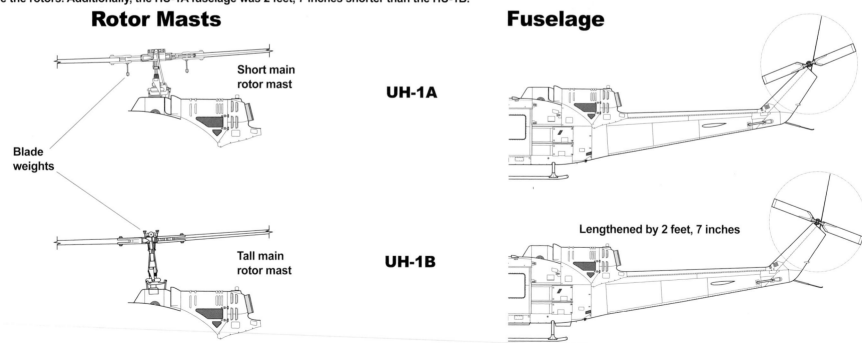

Short main rotor mast

Blade weights

Tall main rotor mast

UH-1A

UH-1B

Lengthened by 2 feet, 7 inches

An HU-1B fitted with 48 ground support rockets hovers during tests at Redstone Arsenal in 1962. The Army contracted with Bell in June 1959 for an improved version of the Huey. The HU-1B was redesignated as the UH-1B after September 1962. This model was powered by the Lycoming T53-L-5 turbine engine rated at 960 shaft horsepower and had its first flight on 27 April 1960. Its rotor mast was 13 inches taller than the HU-1A. Its rotor blades were made of aluminum honeycomb and had a larger 21-inch chord. The fuselage was 2 feet 7 inches longer to accommodate eight passengers or three stretcher casualties. (Army Aviation Museum)

Rotor blades turn as Bell UH-1B 62-1998 perches on a ledge in the desert. A whip antenna for FM radio communications was mounted on top of the tail. VHF navigation antennas, which look like handholds, are located near the rear of the tail boom. (Army Aviation Museum)

A UH-1B converted to a trainer sits on a pad. It is armed with an XM158 rocket launcher, which fired seven 2.75-inch folding-fin rockets. It also has a 7.62mm Minigun on a fixed mount. The electrically-powered Minigun had a variable rate of fire of 2,000 or 4,000 rounds per minute. The same weapons were on the left side. (Army Aviation Museum)

In office from 1965-1967, the Republic of Vietnam's Prime Minister, Nguyễn Cao Kỳ had a personal UH-1B in black. As part of its military aid package, the United States sent many Iroquois helicopters to South Vietnam during the 1960s. Similar to that of the United States, South Vietnam's national insignia featured a star with two yellow bars on each side, all in a red surround with red side bars. Emblazoned on the vertical fin was the flag of the Republic of Vietnam: yellow with three horizontal red stripes. This aircraft has the fuselage code or side No. 62_2054. An external-stores mount is on the side of the cabin, and the engine air intake is the early-type annular combustion scoop. (SSP collection)

A UH-1C hovers over a helipad. It is armed with the nose-mounted XM5 Armament Subsystem that features an M75 40mm grenade launcher in a bulbous turret and M3 24-tube 2.75-inch folding-fin aerial rocket (FFAR) launchers to the sides of the cabin. The UH-1C was designed in 1960 as a transport and gunship version of the Huey, as a reaction to the diminished performance of the UH-1B when armed with weapons. Troops in Vietnam devised the nickname "Huey Hog" for the UH-1C. It was somewhat revolutionary as the first helicopter designed from the start as a gunship. The UH-1C incorporated new rotors with blades with a 27-inch chord, higher-powered T53-L-9 engine, larger tail fin, synchronized elevators, pitot tube relocated to the cockpit roof, as well as other changes and improvements. The result was a faster and more maneuverable Huey that could bring heavy firepower to the fight. The UH-1C served well in its gunship role until the truly revolutionary Bell AH-1 Cobra gunship arrived. (Army Aviation Museum)

UH-1C 64-14102 is armed with the XM5/M5 40mm turret system on the nose. It features a flexible ammunition chute that leads to the turret from the nose. It also is equipped with weapons mounts on the sides of the cabin. Each mount holds an XM134 7.62mm Minigun and an XM157 2.75-inch rocket-launcher pod.

Compared to the UH-1B, the UH-1C had a larger tail pylon, which was mandated by the more powerful engine; larger, synchronized elevators; and a relocated fuel filler, which was moved to the left side of the cabin, aft of the upper rear corner of the sliding door.

This UH-1C Huey Gunship has an inscription on the sliding door to identify the helicopter as a test aircraft of the United States Army Aviation Test Board. It is armed with an XM5 40mm grenade launcher, Miniguns, and XM158 rocket launchers. (Army Aviation Museum)

Although this Huey resembles a UH-1C, it is a UH-1B outfitted as a Huey Hog aircrew trainer. It is armed with an XM5 Armament Subsystem on the nose and M3 2.75-inch FFARs. The UH-1B-style pitot tube is on the left side of the nose. (Army Aviation Museum)

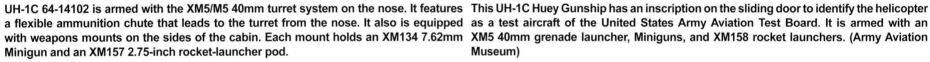

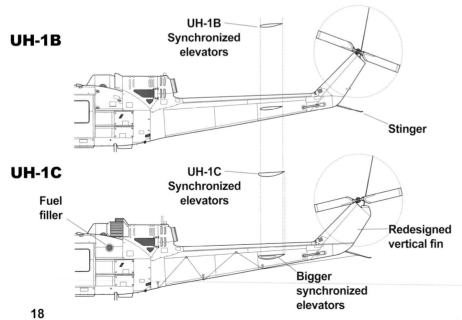

YHU-1D 60-6028, the first of the series, makes its first flight at the Bell Helicopter plant on 16 August 1961 in Hurst, Texas. The YHU-1Ds had 48-foot-long rotor blades with a 21-inch chord. The tail boom was lengthened 18 inches to compensate for the larger blades. (National Archives)

UH-1D 65-9738 sits on a helipad. As seen on this mid-production example, the UH-1Ds retained the nose-mounted pitot tube. The screened dust and particle separators for the engine intake were introduced in 1965. The "towel bar" FM antenna on the roof replaced the nose antennas. (San Diego Air and Space Museum)

U.S. Navy UH-1D 659739 flies out of Naval Air Station Quonset Point, Rhode Island, in 1969. This UH-1D has a tail No. 659739 that equates to a U.S. Air Force serial No. 65-9739. This Huey was assigned to Antarctic Development Squadron 6 (VXE-6) for tests and evaluation. (National Museum of Naval Aviation)

YHU-1D 60-6028, Bell construction No. 701, makes its first flight on 16 August 1961. The YHU-1D, renamed YUH-1D after 18 September 1962, was conceived as a tactical troop transport helicopter, based on the HU-1B but with a significantly enlarged cabin. The cabin was 3 feet, 5 inches longer than the UH-1B. This larger cabin had a floor area 50 percent greater than that of the UH-1B. As a result, the YHU-1D had room for 15 troops or 6 stretcher patients. The Army ordered seven service-test prototypes in July 1960. (National Archives)

UH-1E 151267 flies over a farm community after it was built by Bell. The Marine Corps held a competition in 1962 to select a new assault-support helicopter. Marine Corps planners selected the Bell UH-1B. Modifications were made to the Huey to bring it up to Marine Corps standards. The Marines designated the resulting helicopter as the UH-1E. This helicopter differed from the UH-1B in its all-aluminum construction for corrosion resistance; the use of USMC-compatible communications equipment, which included access to frequencies used by Marines on the ground; a roof-mounted rescue hoist; and a rotor brake to immediately stop rotor movement during shipboard operations. The UH-1E first flew on 7 October 1963. Deliveries began about four months later on 21 February 1964. A total of 192 UH-1Es were completed. The first 34 UH-1Es were based on the UH-1B airframe while later UH-1Es were based on the UH-1C airframe. (National Museum of Naval Aviation)

UH-1E 155349 from Marine Light Helicopter Squadron 267 (HML-267) rests on a helipad at Naval Air Facility China Lake in California on 19 May 1977. The white, zigzag antenna on tail boom is for long-range Low-Frequency Single-Sideband Radio communications. A particle separator, an engine air filter, is placed over the engine air intake. The squadron's ace of spades symbol superimposed with "UV" is on the tail pylon along with its tail code and No. 27. (National Museum of Naval Aviation)

The tail code for Marine Light Helicopter Squadron 367 (HML-367), VT, and No. 15 are marked on the vertical tail of UH-1E 153764 on 5 June 1976. VT-15 is marked on the pilot's door. An "anti-Strela" exhaust shield, nicknamed the "toilet bowl," is on the exhaust to foil anti-aircraft missile attacks. (National Museum of Naval Aviation)

Marine Observation Squadron 6 crewmen prepare Bell UH-1E 151285 for a flight at Camp Pendleton in California on 25 August 1964. The hump visible above the cockpit roof is the rescue hoist that was standard equipment for UH-1Es. The engine air intake lacks a particle separator. (National Museum of Naval Aviation)

22

U.S. Air Force UH-1F 65-7940 flies near farmlands. In June of 1963, the U.S. Air Force contracted with Bell Helicopter to construct the UH-1F. Intended as a support aircraft for missile sites, the UH-1F was also used to transport staff and cargo. This model first flew on 20 February 1964. A total of 119 UH-1Fs were delivered from September 1964 to 1967. Because the Air Force had a large surplus of General Electric T58-GE-3 engines, Bell installed these engines in the UH-1Fs and designed a new fairing to accommodate the engines. The engine exhaust nozzle was directed through the right side of the fairing. The 20th Special Operations Squadron "Green Hornets" used a heavily armed version of the UH-1F; it was designated a UH-1P. (National Archives)

UH-1F 66-1220, which was assigned to Headquarters Command of the U.S. Air Force, is parked at Bollings Air Force Base in the District of Columbia in 1967. On the front door is the insignia of Headquarters Command. The insignia features the U.S. Capitol dome on a blue circle. (National Archives)

Crewmen pose for a portrait with Bell UH-1F 66-1220 parked on a helipad at the Pentagon in 1967. This Huey was painted overall in glossy blue with white on the forward part of the cabin roof. Below the engine exhaust nozzle is a red arrow with the warning, "DANGER / JET BLAST." (National Archives)

UH-1F 65-7940 is parked at Davis-Monthan Air Force Base in Arizona on 24 June 1967. No unit insignia are visible, but a diagonal blue band with white stars in the style seen on Strategic Air Command bombers is on the cabin aft of the sliding door. (National Archives)

A fire extinguisher sits beside UH-1F 65-7940 at Davis Monthan Air Force Base in Arizona on 24 June 1967. The UH-1Fs were equipped with a 48-foot rotor with 21-inch chord. The fuel filler was located high on the left side of the cabin near the General Electric T58-GE-3 engine. (National Archives)

A UH-1H flies over the rural Asian countryside as it serves with the Republic of Vietnam Air Force in 1971. The UH-1H, nicknamed the "Hotel" for the letter H in the military phonetic alphabet, was the version of the Huey that was produced in the greatest numbers. Many UH-1Hs were built from scratch while many UH-1Ds were converted to UH-1H standards with the installation the Lycoming T53-L-13 turbine engine with 1,400 shaft horsepower and other modifications. The pitot tube was moved from the left side of the nose to the cockpit roof. A "towel bar" FM homing antenna was also installed on the roof to the front of the transmission. The first YUH-1H service-test prototype flew in 1966. Production UH-1Hs delivery commenced in September 1967. The U.S. Army alone received some 5,000 of them by 1982. Constant improvements were made to these helicopters to keep them competent for decades. Germany, Japan, Italy, and Taiwan built UH-1Hs under license. (National Archives)

A U.S. Army UH-1H helicopter hovers low over a landing pad. A wire-strike kit, designed to snap high-tension lines should the helicopter fly into them, is attached to the cabin roof and belly. A flightline of UH-60A Blackhawk helicopters is the background. (DVIC)

Bell HH-1H 70-2469 assigned to the 301st Aerospace Rescue and Recovery Squadron (ARRS) at Homestead Air Force Base in Florida, takes off on a training mission in June 1975. The helicopter was light gray with a white cabin roof. (National Archives)

A crewman in a parka inspects a HH-1H assigned to the 1550th Flight Training Squadron at Hill Air Force Base in Utah in 1973. The HH-1H was a UH-1H variant designed for Air Force base-rescue duties. A total of 30 were delivered to the U.S. Air Force between 1970 and 1973. (National Archives)

Capt. John Beurer, right seat, pilots a TH-1H trainer helicopter along with Jeff Cutrell, instructor pilot, at Randolph Air Force Base in Universal City near San Antonio, Texas. It was the first of 24 UH-1Hs modified to train U.S. Air Force helicopter student pilots as a TH-1H. (Master Sgt. Lance Cheung / USAF)

HH-1K 157189 is parked on a hardstand at Marine Corps Air Station (MCAS) Yuma in Arizona on 8 May 1971. "YUMA" is painted in large, black letters on the tail pylon. The tail skid was painted with stripes. The fuel filler was on the left side. (National Museum of Naval Aviation)

Bell HH-1K 157197, assigned to Helicopter Attack Squadron (Light) 5 at Naval Air Station North Island, is parked on a ramp on 14 July 1979. This HH-1K was equipped with a dust and particle separator on the engine-air intake. Low-visibility markings were present. (National Museum of Naval Aviation)

HH-1K 157182 hovers low at Naval Air Station North Island in California on 14 July 1979. The Kilo was equipped with external-weapons mounts and ammunition feed chutes, but machine guns were not installed. The pitot tube is above the cockpit. (National Museum of Naval Aviation)

U.S. Navy HH-1K 157182 prepares for liftoff as it serves with Helicopter Attack Squadron (Light) 5 (HA[L]-5) in July 1979. A rescue hoist is on the cabin roof. The Navy contracted with Bell Helicopter in December 1968 to develop a new search-and-rescue helicopter. It was designated the HH-1K and was nicknamed the "Kilo" for the letter K in the military phonetic alphabet. Based on the Bell UH-1E, the HH-1K was equipped with a new avionics suite. Power was provided by the Lycoming T53-L-13 turbine engine, which has a rating of 1,400 shaft horsepower. Bell began delivery of the HH-1K in May 1970. Three Kilos were shipped to Vietnam in late 1970 to serve with the HA(L)-3 "Seawolves." A total of 27 HH-1Ks were completed. They served with HA(L)-3, the HA(L)-4 "Red Wolves," and the HA(L)-5 "Blue Hawks." (National Museum of Naval Aviation)

U.S. Air Force UH-1N 69-6659, assigned to the 1550th Aircrew Training and Test Wing, flies over a runway at Hill Air Force Base in Utah in 1975. The tail rotor on this model was moved to the right side to compensate for twin-engine torque. Perceiving that a twin-engine Huey could pay dividends in terms of speed and survivability, Bell developed its Model 208. Powered by a Continental XT67 twin engine, the Model 208 first flew in April 1965. The Canadians liked the concept and ordered a Twin Huey from Bell. The Canadian Huey was powered by the Pratt & Whitney Canada PT6T Twin-Pac engine. The U.S. Marine Corps, Navy, and Air Force all ordered a version designated the UH-1N Twin Huey, but the U.S. Army was not interested. (National Archives)

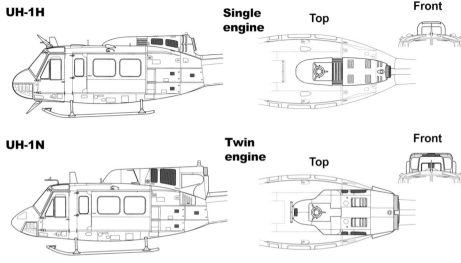

With the Washington Monument in the background, a UH-1N flies above the Potomac River in 1970. The UH-1N featured an extended cabin with doors similar to the UH-1D, a redesigned engine fairing, a more pointed nose, and redesigned chin windows. (National Archives)

These diagrams illustrate the design changes of the UH-1N Twin Huey as compared to the UH-1H. These changes include a redesigned, more-pronounced nose, smaller chin windows and enlarged engine and transmission fairings. Large, dual intakes for the twin-engine pack complete the upgrades.

Marine Corps UH-1N 158260 (1 is missing from the bureau number on the tail) flies near a populated area. The twin exhaust nozzles are located above the rear of the cabin. A red anti-collision light is on the top of the nacelle near the exhausts. A large air scoop is on each side of the fairing alongside the exhausts. (National Museum of Naval Aviation)

U.S. Navy UH-1N 158276 served with Helicopter Combat Support Squadron 16 (HC-16). On the side of the transmission fairing is a large red-and-white sticker to warn of the jet intake danger. The top windows of the cockpit were tinted green in an attempt to reduce glare and heat from the sun through the overheads. (National Museum of Naval Aviation)

A crewman stands in the doorway of a UH-1P Huey. In keeping with the Special Operations role of the UH-1P, it features twin blade antennas on the cabin roof, an exhaust routed through the right side of the engine fairing, and the lack of markings. (Capt. Billie Dee Tedford, via National Museum of the United States Air Force)

With No. 162 stenciled in black on its nose, this UH-1P in Southeast Asia camouflage belongs to the South Vietnam Air Force. A seven-shot 2.75-inch FFAR pod is on the external stores mount. In the background is a Sikorsky H-34 Choctaw helicopter, which also lacks visible markings. (Capt. Billie Dee Tedford, via National Museum of the United States Air Force)

Painted in a Southeast Asia camouflage scheme, a Bell UH-1P helicopter assigned to the 475th Air Base Wing flies over Japan. The aircraft's tail number, 57297, translates to Air Force serial No. 65-2797. Two blade antennas are located on the cockpit roof similar to other UH-1Ps. (DVIC)

33

A U.S. Air Force UH-1P with two blade antennas and lacking visible markings undergoes an engine change at a base in Vietnam. During the Vietnam War, the U.S. Air Force converted approximately 20 of its UH-1Fs to UH-1Ps, which were dedicated to special-operations and psychological-warfare missions. The 20th Special Operations Squadron was the sole user of the UH-1Ps in Vietnam. (Capt. Billie Dee Tedford via National Museum of the United States Air Force)

A UH-1Y lands at Marine Corps Support Facility New Orleans on 9 February 2017. The Bell UH-1Y Venom, sometimes called the Super Huey, represented a major push by the Marine Corps to replace its obsolescent UH-1N Twin Hueys with a state-of-the-art utility helicopter. The UH-1Y is powered by two General Electric T700-GE-401C turboshaft engines. It has a maximum sustained speed of 164 knots and a combat radius of 130 nautical miles. There are provisions to carry Hydra 70 or APKWS II rockets, and two pintle mounts for machine guns. Other upgrades include a four-bladed, all-composite rotor; improved avionics; and an up-to-date forward-looking infrared (FLIR) system. (DVIDS)

Members of Marine Light Attack Helicopter Squadron (HMLA) 469 unload a UH-1Y Venom at Marine Corps Air Station Iwakuni in Japan on 16 September 2016. A 21-inch insert between the cockpit and auxiliary doors provides extra cargo space. (DVIDS)

The aircrew of a UH-1Y from Marine Light Attack Helicopter Squadron 267, 3rd Marine Aircraft Wing, stand by during stop to refuel at Kadena Air Base in Okinawa on 14 February 2017. A cable cutter is mounted above the center of the windscreen. (DVIDS)

UH-1Y 168943 of Marine Light Attack Helicopter Squadron 369 lands at Marine Corps Air Station Camp Pendleton on 4 November 2016. Below the cockpit is the dome-shaped Brite Star II FLIR. The lower cable cutter is located aft of the Brite Star II FLIR. (DVIDS)

A UH-1Y Venom from Marine Aviation Weapons and Tactics Squadron One (MAWTS-1) kicks up debris in October 2016. Compared with the UH-1N that the Venom replaced, the latter has 170 percent more payload and 50 percent more range and speed. (DVIDS)

Civilians tour a UH-1Y Venom from Marine Light Attack Helicopter Squadron 267, 13th Marine Expeditionary Unit, in San Francisco on 6 October 2012. The Venom was shackled to the flight deck of the *Wasp*-class amphibious assault ship USS *Makin Island* (LHD-8) as part of static-display tours during Fleet Week. (Sgt. Christopher O'Quin / USMC)

A U.S. Army UH-1B with a door gunner flies on a mission armed with a XM16 package of quad M60 machine guns and rocket pods. Only three years after production of the UH-1 series began in 1960, the United States began a troop buildup in Vietnam. Shortly thereafter, the first Hueys were sent into combat. The versatile Huey was utilized for troop insertion, medevac, gunship, reconnaissance and resupply. Much as the jeep became linked to GIs in WWII, the Huey became iconic of U.S. troops of all branches of service in Vietnam. Ultimately, more than 16,000 Hueys were produced over a span of five decades. Despite its service in every U.S. conflict since Vietnam, the Huey remains firmly linked to U.S. involvement in Southeast Asia. (Army Aviation Museum)

Although the XM5 grenade launcher on the chin gives the impression that this is a UH-1C Huey Hog, it actually is UH-1A 58-2083 with the XM5 Armament Subsystem installed. It was parked at Springfield Armory in Massachusetts in August 1962. All UH-1A models have a short rotor mast compared to later models. (National Archives)

The XM5 Armament Subsystem comprised an M75 40mm grenade launcher in a flexible, powered mount in a bulbous turret. The launcher fired up to 220 antipersonnel fragmentation grenades per minute to a maximum range of 4,920 feet. (National Archives)

The M75 40mm grenade launcher was fed ammunition from a magazine in the nose through a flexible chute. A gunner fired the weapon using a control mechanism, or the pilot could fire the grenade launcher when it was in a fixed position. (National Archives)

39

U.S. Army UH-1B 60-3589 is armed with the XM6 quad machine-gun system as it demonstrates its firepower at the 44th annual meeting of the Ordnance Association at Aberdeen Proving Ground in Maryland on 4 October 1962. (National Archives)

Specialists Almer Kelson, left, and Gordon Johnson, right, of the Utility Tactical Transport (UTT) Company, based at Tân Sơn Nhứt Air Base in the Republic of Vietnam sight-in an eight-pack 2.75-inch Folding Fin Aerial Rocket (FFAR) multiple launcher on a UH-1B on 21 February 1963. (National Archives)

A gunner in the left seat of a UH-1B demonstrates the reflex sight of the XM5 armament subsystem at Springfield Armory in Massachusetts in 1962. The sight was on flexible arms and could be pushed toward the cockpit ceiling when not in use. The pilot could also fire the weapon in fixed position using an XM6 reflex sight. The system's maximum capacity was either 150 or 302 rounds of 40mm grenade ammunition. (National Archives)

Specialists Almer Kelson, left, and Gordon Johnson, right, of the Utility Tactical Transport (UTT) Company perform maintenance on the generator of a UH-1B at Tân Sơn Nhứt Air Base on 21 February 1963. To the right of Kelson's knee is the oil tank with a yellow filler cap and blue oil-line connections. (National Archives)

Spc. 4th Class Weldon Reynolds, left, makes an adjustment while Spc. 5th Class Joseph McGurk, right, slides a 2.75-inch folding-fin aerial rocket into a tube of an eight-pack launcher at the UTT Company's area at Tân Sơn Nhứt Air Base on 21 February 1963. (National Archives)

Spc. 4th Class Glenn Martin of the UTT Company at Tân Sơn Nhứt Airbase in the Republic of Vietnam loads an M1919 .30-caliber Browning machine gun on an improvised mount on a UH-1A Huey on 21 February 1963. A large box of ammunition is inside the cargo compartment. The ammo belt is routed through holes in the floor and fuselage to the external machine gun. (National Archives)

U.S. Army UH-1A 59-1695, assigned to the UTT Company, conducts a ground-support mission over South Vietnam on 21 February 1963. This Huey was armed with eight-pack 2.75-inch FFARs and M1919 .30-caliber Browning machine gun fixed mounts. (National Archives)

UH-1B 62-1988, right, and another UH-1B depart the landing zone after they delivered Pathfinders of the 11th Air Assault Division during an air-mobility symposium at Fort Benning in Georgia in August 1963. The final Pathfinder unit was deactivated from the 82nd Combat Aviation Brigade at Fort Bragg on 24 February 2017. (National Archives)

An XM16 Armament Subsystem with an XM157 7-shot 2.75-inch FFAR pod are mounted on the right side of a UH-1B helicopter at Aberdeen Proving Ground on 8 June 1964. Flexible feed chutes supplied 7.62mm ammunition to the two M60C 7.62mm machine guns. The two dark-colored objects on the feed chutes above the rocket pod are cartridge drives. The blue warheads on the 2.75-inch folding-fin aerial rockets signify inert practice rounds. (Military History Institute)

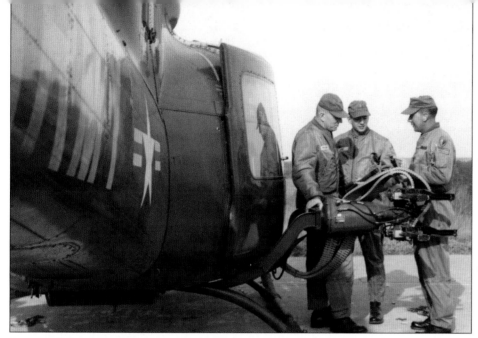

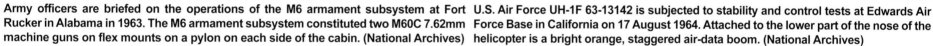

Army officers are briefed on the operations of the M6 armament subsystem at Fort Rucker in Alabama in 1963. The M6 armament subsystem constituted two M60C 7.62mm machine guns on flex mounts on a pylon on each side of the cabin. (National Archives)

U.S. Air Force UH-1F 63-13142 is subjected to stability and control tests at Edwards Air Force Base in California on 17 August 1964. Attached to the lower part of the nose of the helicopter is a bright orange, staggered air-data boom. (National Archives)

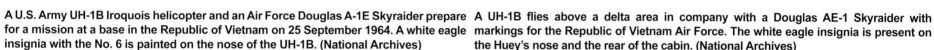

A U.S. Army UH-1B Iroquois helicopter and an Air Force Douglas A-1E Skyraider prepare for a mission at a base in the Republic of Vietnam on 25 September 1964. A white eagle insignia with the No. 6 is painted on the nose of the UH-1B. (National Archives)

A UH-1B flies above a delta area in company with a Douglas AE-1 Skyraider with markings for the Republic of Vietnam Air Force. The white eagle insignia is present on the Huey's nose and the rear of the cabin. (National Archives)

Bell UH-1D helicopters are lined up on the amphibious assault ship USS *Iwo Jima* (LPH-2) off the coast of Vietnam and await orders to move to their land base on 12 April 1965. On top of the crates to the far left, a cameraman films the takeoffs. (National Archives)

Sgt. Dennis Troxel jumps out of a UH-1B to prime the M60C machine guns during a mission in Vietnam on 12 September 1965. Troxel, a 25th Infantry Division soldier, was a volunteer "shotgun rider" in this 179th Aviation Company Huey. (National Archives)

A UH-1D airlifts troops from the 4th Battalion, 503rd Infantry, position to the 173rd Airborne Brigade's forward base camp after a successful search-and-destroy mission near Xuân Lộc, Republic of Vietnam, on 1 September 1966. (National Archives)

A casualty is loaded into a UH-1B on 21 May 1966 during Operation Wahiawa, a 25th Infantry Division search-and-destroy mission in Hậu Nghĩa Province. Medical evacuations (medevacs) were an iconic mission of UH-1s in Vietnam. (National Archives)

U.S. Army UH-1Bs are serviced at a base in Vietnam on 19 May 1966. The upper rear parts of the cabins were painted orange. Between the helicopters a service cart carries a fuel or oil tank. To the right is a tricycle service car. (National Archives)

A UH-1B helicopter brings supplies to Camp Dean, a radio relay station on Núi Bà Đen ("Black Virgin Mountain") in South Vietnam's Tây Ninh Province in early June 1966. To the left is a sandbagged bunker built atop a large rock, which features graffiti from the camp builders. (National Archives)

Elements of the 25th Infantry Division are transported in UH-1s during Operation Fort Smith, near An Bình hamlet in the area of the division's base camp at Củ Chi, in early June 1966. In the foreground is the barrel of a door-mounted M60 7.62mm machine gun. (National Archives)

A UH-1D with an open sliding door and the auxiliary door removed flies low over rice paddies during Operation Fort Smith. A silhouette of a white bear is on the rear of the sliding door. The tail skid is painted yellow. (National Archives)

Troops from the 3rd Brigade, 25th Infantry Division load C-ration boxes into the cabin of a UH-1D on 31 July 1966. In Vietnam, Hueys airlifted supplies wherever needed and performed a role akin to flying jeeps or cargo trucks. (National Archives)

Troops from 4th Battalion, 503rd Infantry, 173rd Airborne Brigade scramble from a UH-1D at the brigade's forward base camp in Xuân Lộc in the Republic of Vietnam after a successful search-and-destroy mission on 1 September 1966. (National Archives)

During Operation Kamuala, an operation by 2nd Battalion, 14th Infantry, 25th Infantry Division, to interdict food supplies to the enemy, a soldier escorts a suspected Việt Cộng family to UH-1D 65-9608 for evacuation on 27 September 1966. (National Archives)

This UH-1B of the 336th Aviation Company, 13th Aviation Battalion, 1st Aviation Brigade, crashed during a test flight at Sóc Trăng in the Republic of Vietnam on 2 October 1966. With a missing nose enclosure, the avionics equipment is exposed. (National Archives)

As a UH-1D lifts off to assault Việt Cộng forces, troops from Company C, 503rd Airborne Infantry, wait to be picked up by the next Huey during Operation Meridian, a search-and-destroy operation, about 465 miles northwest of Biên Hòa on 10 November 1966. (National Archives)

During another phase of Operation Meridian, soldiers of Company B, 2nd Battalion, 503rd Airborne Infantry, 173rd Airborne Brigade (Separate), advance through a clearing while four UH-1Ds in camouflage paint schemes approach to land on 10 November 1966. (National Archives)

A Huey helicopter undergoes repairs on the deck of the floating aircraft maintenance depot USNS *Corpus Christi Bay* anchored in Cam Ranh Bay on 12 November 1966. Large cranes were available to lift engines and other heavy components. The rotor has been lifted off the rotor mast, but the main rotor tie-down remains tied around the tail boom. The ship's helipad is marked-off in white paint. (National Archives)

47

A member of the Civilian Irregular Defense Group (CIDG), South Vietnamese minority population paramilitary auxiliary troops, jumps from a UH-1D at the start of a search-and-destroy mission northwest of Tuy Hòa on 23 November 1966. An M60D 7.62mm machine gun is installed on an M23 mount. (National Archives)

A Navy UH-1B Helicopter from Attack Squadron (Light) 3 "Seawolves" is armed with quad 7.62mm machine guns and seven-shot 2.75-inch FFAR pods at Vĩnh Long on 12 January 1967. Navy Hueys assisted riverine patrol craft during Việt Cộng interdictions on waterways. (National Museum of Naval Aviation)

An AN/ARC-122 Communication Center inside a UH-1B has been prepared for a mission at Landing Zone Hammond in the Republic of Vietnam on 9 February 1967. Also part of this installation was an RT-246 VHF low-band radio set. Bell Hueys were highly adaptable to multiple roles as communications and command helicopters. (National Archives)

A groundcrew moves a UH-1B assigned to the 175th Aviation Company to the heliport at Tân Sơn Nhứt Air Base in Saigon in February 1967. Its cabin is marked with "Maverick" and "36." It was airlifted to Saigon by a CH-47 Chinook from Long Bình Post for shipment to the United States for a rebuild. (National Archives)

An AN/ASC-6 airborne command radio set is installed in the cabin of a Bell UH-1B Iroquois helicopter at an unidentified base in the Republic of Vietnam on 25 May 1967. "PILOT / M. Bennett" is marked on the door post toward the right. (National Archives)

"CHUCK CRUSHER II," a UH-1C from the 3rd Platoon, 114th Assault Helicopter Company, is armed with an M75 40mm grenade launcher in the XM5 Armament Subsystem and M3 12-tube, 2.75-inch FFAR launchers. (Eugene Schwanebeck)

During Operation Pershing, a May 1967 search-and-destroy mission in Bình Định Province in the Republic of Vietnam, troops of Company A, 1st Battalion, 7th Cavalry, receive a resupply from a UH-1D helicopter. The unit was attached to the 1st Cavalry Division (Airmobile). (National Archives)

49

Bell UH-1s sometimes distributed propaganda flyers in the continued psychological operations (psy-ops) conducted by the military and intelligence agencies. Crewmen in this UH-1D toss handfuls of pamphlets out of the door in June 1967. (National Archives)

Many UH-1s of the 335th Assault Helicopter Company transport the 4th Battalion, 503rd Infantry, to a landing zone 20 kilometers northwest Tuy Hòa for the kickoff of Operation Bolling, a search-and-destroy mission, on 17 September 1967. (National Archives)

A mix of UH-1Ds and -Hs from Company A, 2nd Battalion, 8th Cavalry, 1st Air Cavalry Division, retrieve infantrymen from a search-and-destroy operation some 5 kilometers southwest of Landing Zone Uplift in Vietnam in late October 1967. (National Archives)

Two UH-1Ds deliver troops in a clearing in Vietnam in October 1967. The nearer Huey has No. 644 stenciled on the tail fin. The utility door to the front of the sliding door has been detached. The sliding door was easily removed on UH-1Ds and UH-1Hs. (National Archives)

A 9th Infantry Division UH-1D is almost completely surrounded by water as it rests on its helipad at Tân An, Vietnam, on 26 October 1967. In the background is a truck-mounted 1,500 gallon-per-hour ERDLator. It was used to make potable water from local water sources such as the pools around the Huey. (National Archives)

A UH-1D flies alongside a Huey with a door-mounted M60 during Operation Francis Marion, which transpired from 5 April through 12 October 1967. The operation aimed to confine the North Vietnamese Army near Ia Đrăng. The youth and inexperience of many of the troops inserted by helicopter led to criticism. (National Archives)

51

A crewman in a U.S. Navy UH-1B fires a twin M1919 .30-caliber Browning machine gun installation at Việt Cộng forces in the Mekong Delta in November 1967. This gun mount was installed in the lead helicopter of Helicopter Attack (Light) Squadron 3. (National Museum of Naval Aviation)

Helicopter Attack Squadron (Light) 3 "Seawolves" maintenance personnel service two Hueys on 15 November 1967. The helicopter on the right is marked for Detachment 1 on the nose. These Hueys assisted in Operation Game Warden in the Mekong Delta. (National Museum of Naval Aviation)

In October 1967, a UH-1D hovers next to a helicopter landing platform, developed for use in the swampy terrain of the Mekong Delta in South Vietnam. The platform was fabricated from aluminum tubes, with a chain-link platform surface. The platform was 22 feet in diameter, weighed 900 pounds, and could be airlifted to the desired location by helicopter. It also was intended that the platform could serve as a command post or first-aid station. (National Archives)

Two U.S. Navy Hueys, which includes one numbered 033 in the background, patrol the Mekong Delta in support of Operation Game Warden on 15 November 1967. The operation was an interdiction campaign against the Việt Cộng in the Delta's waterways. Sunlight falls on the pilot's instrument panel. (National Museum of Naval Aviation)

An Army UH-1H lands on a U.S. Navy armored troop carrier in the Mekong Delta in the Republic of Vietnam in 1967. The UH-1H "Slick" is marked with No. 86 on the tail fin. The boat was assigned to River Assault Flotilla 1. The flotilla's modified ships and boats supported an Army infantry brigade and an artillery battalion. (National Archives)

Troops begin to scramble out of a U.S. Army UH-1H from Troop C, 7th Squadron, 1st Cavalry Regiment (Airmobile), 1st Aviation Brigade, at a landing zone in Tân An Province in the Republic of Vietnam on 14 April 1968. Yellow Cavalry markings are on the nose and roof. (National Archives)

Grunts load cases of C-rations and ginger ale into a UH-1H with a rooftop pitot tube at Fire Base Berchtesgaden, west of Huế, during Operation Somerset Plain in early August 1968. The sliding and auxiliary doors have been removed. An M60D 7.62mm machine gun is installed on an M23 mount. (National Archives)

A UH-1B gunship assigned to Detachment 3 of Helicopter Attack (Light) Squadron 3 fires a 2.75-inch FFAR during a Việt Cộng force engagement along the Cổ Chiên River around May 1968. The Huey flew in support of Navy river patrol boats (PBRs) in the Mekong Delta in South Vietnam. (National Museum of Naval Aviation)

A Marine Corps UH-1E assigned to Marine Aircraft Group 16 (MAG-16) backs out of a revetment at the Marble Mountain Air Facility on 28 September 1968 in Đà Nẵng, Republic of Vietnam. It is armed with seven-shot rocket pods mounted on the TK-2 Armament Subsystem. (National Museum of Naval Aviation)

Members of Detachment 1 (Det-1) of the Helicopter Attack (Light) Squadron 3 (HAL-3) "Seawolves" perform maintenance and repairs to the engine and the rotor assemblies of one of the unit's UH-1Bs around May 1968. "DET-1" is written on the nose in an Asian-inspired script. The HAL-3 emblem features a standing wolf that holds a trident and a shield with a black ace. (National Museum of Naval Aviation)

This upside-down U.S. Marine Corps UH-1E crashed when it ran out of fuel, a short distance south of the Naval Support Activity (NSA) Station Hospital at Đà Nẵng in 1968. While four of the helicopter occupants were injured, there were no fatalities. (National Museum of Naval Aviation)

While a UH-1B is already parked on USS *Garrett County* (LST-786), a Navy UH-1B prepares to land on the ship in Vietnamese waters. The tank landing ship provided a mobile support base for Navy helicopters and patrol boats during Việt Cộng interdiction activities along the waterways of the Mekong Delta. (National Museum of Naval Aviation)

A U.S. Air Force UH-1F lifts off from a helipad as it serves as a trainer with the 3630th Flying Training Wing at Sheppard Air Force Base in Texas in August 1969. The helicopter was painted overall in Dark Gloss Blue with a Gloss White cabin roof and a yellow band on the tail boom. (National Archives)

A short-fuselage UH-1C Iroquois helicopter hovers low over a hardstand at an airbase. C-model Hueys are identifiable by the cambered, broad-chord vertical fin and the white position lights on both sides of the aft tail boom rather than the trailing edge of the fin like most Hueys. XM159 2.75-inch FFAR pods are mounted on the pylons. (Bell Helicopters)

A tractor pulls UH-1D 66-0971 from the hold of a C-124 cargo aircraft for reassembly at the 520th Aircraft Processing Plant at Tân Sơn Nhứt Air Force Base in late July 1969. The detached tail boom rests on a plywood roof cradle. (National Archives)

A tractor tows UH-1D 66-0971 from a C-124 Globemaster II to the 520th Aircraft Processing Plant at Tân Sơn Nhứt, where the helicopter will be reassembled for service. (National Archives)

A tractor pulls UH-1D 66-0971 into a revetment at Tân Sơn Nhứt in July 1969. The helicopter's ground-handling wheels are installed on the landing skids. Assembled Hueys are located to the right and in the background. (National Archives)

Finally, UH-1D 66-0971 is parked in a revetment at Tân Sơn Nhứt to await reassembly in late July 1969. A bracket fabricated from angle irons was attached to the tail boom and the rear of the cabin to securely hold the tail boom for shipment. (National Archives)

A UH-1D or -H from the 336th Aviation Company sprays a defoliant on a strip of jungle in the Mekong Delta on 26 July 1969. A controversial mission Hueys performed was to spray defoliants to remove leaves from trees and rob the enemy of the concealment provided by Vietnam's lush vegetation. (National Archives)

An Army UH-1D has been outfitted with the Firefly system of spotlights to illuminate potential targets at night in Vietnam in August of 1969. An M2 .50-caliber Browning machine gun was installed on a heavy-duty bracket bolted to the floor of the cargo compartment. (National Archives)

A U.S. Navy UH-1, armed with the XM16 quad machine gun system and M158 seven-tube 2.75-inch FFARs, flies over the Cửa Lớn River aft of U.S. Navy Patrol Craft Fast, commonly called a Swift Boat, in July 1969. Navy helicopters and riverine patrol boats worked as teams to scout and remove Việt Cộng and their sympathizers from the coastal waterways of Vietnam. (National Museum of Naval Aviation)

The nickname "HOGHEAD II" is painted on the left-forward door of this UH-1C Heavy Hog from the 114th Assault Helicopter Company. The Huey is armed with an M75 40mm grenade launcher and M3 12-tube, 2.75-inch FFAR launchers. (Eugene Schwanebeck)

The UH-1H assigned to the commanding officer of the 11th Combat Aviation Battalion in Vietnam was armed with an M60D 7.62mm machine gun on an M23 mount in September 1969. An ammunition box and flexible ammo chute are connected. (National Archives)

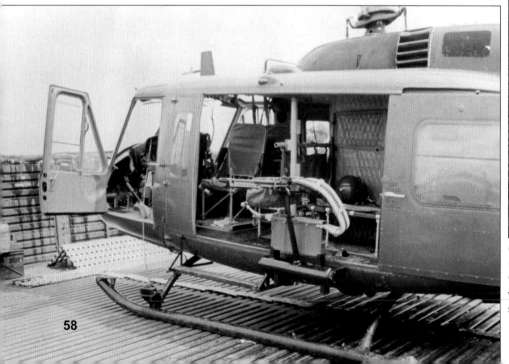

"LEAD" is painted on the upper part of the nose of this UH-1C Heavy Hog from the 114th Assault Helicopter Company. The nickname of this particular helicopter was "HOGHEAD." It appears to have been the predecessor of "HOGHEAD II." A cobra snake was painted on each side of the nose, and the turret of the 40mm grenade launcher had shark's teeth and eyes painted on it. (Eugene Schwanebeck)

Members of Company C, 2nd Battalion, 3rd Infantry, 199th Light Infantry Brigade, along with the crew of an M113 armored cavalry assault vehicle (ACAV), take a defensive posture while a UH-1H with M60D machine guns in the doors hovers overhead near Long Binh in the Republic of Vietnam on 6 October 1969. (National Archives)

The same unit prepares to move out behind the cover of an M113 ACAV as a U.S. Army UH-1H passes above near Long Binh on 6 October 1969. Inside the cabin of the Huey, a crewman mans the M60D machine gun. (National Archives)

A UH-1H helicopter inserts troops from the 101st Airborne Division in a small clearing during a sweep of an area south of the Demilitarized Zone (DMZ) between North Vietnam and South Vietnam on 16 October 1969. M60D 7.62mm machine guns of the M23 Helicopter Armament Subsystem are visible on each side of the Huey. A landing light is in the lowered position below the nose. (National Archives)

UH-1Hs of the U.S. Army's 1st Signal Brigade line up at Nha Trang Airbase in the Republic of Vietnam in November of 1969. The 1st Signal Brigade's insignia is painted on the nose of the second Huey. These Hueys transported Signal personnel and equipment throughout II Corps Area. (National Archives)

TH-1F 66-1250, assigned to Air Force Headquarters Command, flies past the Lincoln Memorial in 1969. On the pilot's door is the insignia of Headquarters Command. The insignia features a shield with the U.S. Capitol dome in white within a blue circle with 13 gold bars around the perimeter. (National Archives)

A UH-1H brings a cargo shipment of steel cables to members of the 47th Infantry Regiment during the U.S. incursion into Cambodia in May of 1970. Several M113 armored personnel carriers, which includes an ACAV (armored cavalry assault vehicle), are parked at the site. (National Archives)

A gunner in the open cargo door of a UH-1B Huey mans an M60 machine gun during a patrol of the South Vietnamese waterways on 29 June 1970. The insignia of Helicopter Attack Squadron (Light) 3 "Seawolves" is painted on the nose of the Huey. (National Museum of Naval Aviation)

A door gunner of a Royal Australian Air Force (RAAF) UH-1H of No. 9 Squadron looks down at the camera while the helicopter lands at the foot of the Núi Thị Vải hills complex on 20 July 1970. The RAAF's No. 9 Squadron was involved in Vietnam from 3 May 1966 until 17 December 1971. (National Archives)

Troops from Company B, 2nd Royal Australian Army Regiment, board a UH-1D helicopter from No. 9 Squadron of the RAAF at a site along the foot of the Núi Thị Vải hills complex in the Republic of Vietnam on 20 July 1970. (National Archives)

A UH-1H assigned to No. 9 Helicopter Squadron, RAAF has begun to lift off from the landing site near the Núi Thị Vải hills on 20 July 1970. A flight crewman mans an M60D 7.62mm machine gun. (National Archives)

A UH-1H from No. 9 Helicopter Squadron of the RAAF clears the ground and moves forward during a mission on 20 July 1970. "RAAF" is marked on the tail boom, and a red, white, and dark blue flash is painted on the tail fin. Six No. 9 Squadron members were killed in action during the war. (National Archives)

Soldiers from the 2nd Royal Australian Regiment load rations aboard a UH-1H from No. 9 Squadron for transport to the 2nd Battalion, Australian and New Zealand Army Corps (ANZAC) on 21 July 1970 at Núi Đất, Republic of Vietnam. (National Archives)

Troops from the 2nd ANZAC Battalion load rations and other supplies into the cargo compartment of a RAAF UH-1H Huey at Núi Đất on 21 July 1970. The Royal Australian Air Force also operated Bell UH-1D helicopters during the Vietnam War. (National Archives)

An aircrewman from the No. 9 Squadron removes the bullet trap, a safety device, from a Minigun on a Huey at Núi Đất on 22 July 1970. On the pilot's door is the No. 9 Squadron insignia, which features a white duck's head over a blue crown. (National Archives)

Dressed for the tropical heat of a July in Vietnam, a maintenance technician from No. 9 Squadron, RAAF, troubleshoots a 7.62mm Minigun. The Minigun had jammed during a recent mission. The pilot is positioned in a armored seat. (National Archives)

Two men from No. 9th Squadron load 2.75-inch FFARs into an M158 2.75-inch rocket pod at the base of No. 9 Squadron. Twin M60 7.62mm machine guns are mounted on a pedestal attached to the external stores pylon. (National Archives)

An aircrewman from No. 9 Squadron prepares to embark on a mission. The Australians sometimes emplaced two external stores pylons on each side of their UH-1D and -H gunships. One pylon was for a Minigun and one for rockets. (National Archives)

A member of No. 9 Squadron, RAAF, loads 7.62mm ammunition into the boxes at Núi Đất on 22 July 1970. A bank of four 7.62mm ammunition boxes fed the two General Electric M134 Miniguns mounted on Hueys. The Miniguns could go through a lot of ammunition in a hurry at a rate of fire of 2,000 or 4,000 rounds per minute per gun. (National Archives)

Soldiers from Company E, 4th Battalion, 21st Infantry, unload a precious cargo of cola and beer cases from a Huey at Landing Zone Charlie Brown, southeast of Đức Phổ in Quảng Ngãi Province, South Vietnam, on 9 July 1970. Beer and soft drinks were welcome morale builders in the tropical heat. (National Archives)

Two U.S. Army UH-1Hs, including serial No. 66-1058 in the foreground, engage in disaster relief for victims of a large earthquake at the airstrip at Anta in Peru on 22 June 1970. Both Hueys had orange areas on the fuselages for high visibility. (National Archives)

Several members of the 162nd Aviation Company (Combat Assault) remove the mount for an M134 Minigun on a Huey at Cần Thơ in the Republic of Vietnam in July 1970. The man to the left holds the gun mount and adapter. Below the mount is a seven-tube 2.75-inch FFAR launcher without a shroud. This type of launcher was easier to repair than a podded FFAR launcher if one or more of the tubes became damaged or unserviceable. (National Archives)

A UH-1D, tail No. 15334, lifts off after it delivered a load of baggage at Marine Corps Air Station El Toro in California in July of 1970. Steps were attached below the cargo doors because it served as a presidential support helicopter. (National Museum of Naval Aviation)

A UH-1M, an upgraded UH-1C with T53-L-13 engine, of the 11th Combat Aviation Group is equipped with the Hughes INFANT (Iroquois Night Fighter And Night Tracker) with an image-intensifier scope and infrared video camera at Phú Lợi, about 20km north of Saigon, in September 1970. (National Archives)

A UH-1C from the 162nd Aviation Company (Combat Assault) is parked on the flightline at Cần Thơ Army Airfield in the Republic of Vietnam in 1970. The helicopter is armed with the M21 armament subsystem, which includes two M158 2.75-inch FFAR launchers and two Miniguns. Jutting from the sides of the rear of the tail boom are white position lights. White position lights located on the aft tail boom are distinct to C-model Hueys rather than on the trailing edge of the fin similar to other UH-1s. At the top of the tail fin is the right-angle final-drive gearbox and shaft as well as the tail rotor. (National Archives)

The engine and transmission fairings are removed for maintenance from this short-fuselage UH-1C from the 162nd Aviation Company (Combat Assault) at Cần Thơ in 1970. The engine fairing was split at the top fore and aft with each section hinged at the rear. This UH-1C is identifiable by the Bell 540 "door hinge" high-speed rotor. The rotor blades droop equally on each side of the rotor head since the rotor head plate bends at the mast. Other Hueys have blades that angle up a few degrees from each other in their semi-rigid rotor heads. (National Archives)

The XM93 armament system provided door mounts for two M134 7.62mm Miniguns in long-fuselage Hueys. The Minigun was on a flexible mount, with two hand grips. Connected to a collector tray below the gun cradle is a flexible hose to eject spent cases. (National Archives)

A crew chief greases a component on the rotor head of a Huey assigned to the 162nd Aviation Company (Combat Assault) at the Cần Thơ Army Airfield in 1970. Above his head is the rotor hub. Below the rotor head is the transmission. Even a relatively small helicopter such as the Huey had a maze of hydraulic and electrical lines, control linkages and intricate mechanisms. (National Archives)

Three UH-1 Hueys assigned to the 101st Assault Helicopter Battalion, 101st Airborne Division (Airmobile), approach to land with troops of the 502nd Infantry at a fire-support base southwest of Huế in the Republic of Vietnam in 1970. (National Archives)

Soldiers load 2.75-inch FFARs into an M158 launcher on a short-fuselage Huey. Above the launcher is an M134 7.62mm Minigun and the flex chute for the Minigun ammunition. Belted 7.62mm ammo hangs from the bottom of the flex chute. (National Archives)

Two U.S. Air Force UH-1N Twin Hueys fly over a coastline in 1970. The helicopters are painted in the Southeast Asia camouflage scheme and carry no visible branch or unit markings. The U.S. Air Force, Marines and Navy all used the UH-1N Twin Huey. (National Archives)

67

A Huey helicopter has landed in a very small clearing to extract a team from Company C, 1st Battalion, 327th Airborne Infantry, 101st Airborne Division, and return them to Fire Support Base Birmingham, south of Huế, South Vietnam, on 15 April 1971. The terrain of Vietnam and the ill-defined front made the helicopters invaluable. (National Archives)

A U.S. Air Force UH-1N is parked on a hardstand at Edwards Air Force Base in California on 3 June 1971. The helicopter has the M93 armament system with two door-mounted M134 7.62mm Miniguns. An M157 2.75-inch FFAR launcher is on the external pylon. (National Archives)

A long-fuselage VIP UH-1H assigned to Continental Army Command at Fort Monroe in Virginia is parked at Fort George G. Meade in Maryland on 9 June 1971. Upholstered seats are installed in the cabin. A suit rack with coat hangers attached is located in the rear of the cabin. A "towel rack" FM homing antenna is on the roof. (National Archives)

Carpet is installed in the interior of the UH-1H of Continental Army Command from Fort Monroe. Soundproof materials are installed on the ceiling of the cabin that matches the dark-yellow seat upholstery. A cabinet and curtain are to the front for VIP travel. (National Archives)

A UH-1N is armed with an M93 armament subsystem, which features a door-mounted Minigun, at the Test Center at Edwards Air Force Base in California on 1 July 1971. Mounted on the pylon is a LAU-59/A 2.75-inch FFAR launcher, which is the Air Force designation for the seven-shot pod. (National Archives)

The crew of this UH-1H poses with their aircraft and its medevac gear during a demonstration in April 1972 at Fort Sam Houston in San Antonio, Texas. The soldiers and aircraft were assigned to the 507th Medical Company (Air Ambulance). The 507th pioneered the application of medevac procedures learned in Vietnam to civilian needs such as traffic accidents. (National Archives)

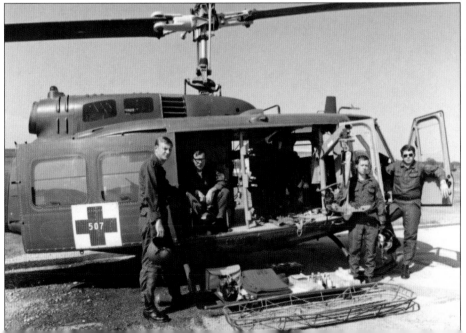

The rescue hoist in a Bell UH-1N Twin Huey helicopter is deployed at the Air Force Flight Test Center at Edwards Air Force Base in California on 29 July 1971. It incorporates a boom mounted on a vertical stanchion. Suspended from the boom is a round, yellow handle. Below the handle is the rescue hook with a safety latch. (National Archives)

Soldiers from the 172nd Infantry Brigade load an Akhio sled, a U.S. Army rescue sled, into the cabin of a long-fuselage UH-1 during a winter training exercise at Fort Richardson in Alaska in January of 1972. The helicopter was painted in a high-visibility scheme. (National Archives)

Civilian evacuees sprint to a long-fuselage UH-1H – identifiable by the rooftop pitot tube and a "towel rack" FM homing antenna – at Tencza Compound in Kon Tum, in the Central Highlands of South Vietnam, on 29 April 1972. The Huey airlifted them to safety at a time when North Vietnamese forces were closing in on the city. (National Archives)

A UH-1N Twin Huey is parked during an all-weather test at Eielson Air Force Base in Alaska on 14 January 1972. Olive Drab covers are installed over the rotor blades and the pitot tube above the cockpit. Despite the Arctic location, Southeast Asia camouflage is applied. (National Archives)

UH-1N 158276 of Marine Light Attack Helicopter Squadron 167 (HMA-167) flies near Camp Lejeune in North Carolina on 4 January 1973. This Twin Huey crashed on 16 August 2007 at Yuma Proving Grounds in Arizona; only one of the five occupants survived. (National Museum of Naval Aviation)

The aircrew of a USAF HH-1H helicopter scramble to their helicopter during a training exercise at Hill Air Force Base in Utah on 22 February 1973. The Huey is painted light gray with a white roof. The aft end of the engine fairing and cabin is bright yellow. (National Archives)

A U.S. Air Force HH-1H rescue helicopter flies over a snowy forest during a training exercise out of Hill Air Force Base in Utah in February of 1972. (National Archives)

Aircrew members check the rescue hoist of HH-1H 70-2465 before a rescue training exercise. Tail number 02465 refers to the helicopter's serial No. 70-2465. The orange band around the cabin is edged in black. (National Archives)

A Bell HH-1H helicopter has a load braced and attached to the rescue-boom hook at the Flight Test Center at Edwards Air Force Base in California on 14 February 1973. An air-data boom is attached to the nose for flight-test purposes. (National Archives)

A U.S. Army UH-1H Huey helicopter is parked at Tân Sơn Nhứt Air Base in March 1973. It has been placed at the disposal of the International Commission of Control and Supervision (ICCS), which supervised the implementation of the Paris Peace Accords in Vietnam. (National Archives)

Several U.S. Hueys have "ICCS" markings on them while they are parked on a flightline at Tân Sơn Nhứt Air Base in the Republic of Vietnam on 24 March 1973. To foil shoulder-launched anti-aircraft guided missiles, all of these aircraft have the anti-Strela "toilet bowl" shields on the engine exhausts. (National Archives)

A line of five UH-1 Iroquois helicopters arrived to pick up American prisoners of war being released from captivity at Lộc Ninh in the Republic of Vietnam in 1973. (DVIC)

A U.S. Air Force Twin Huey flies over the Jefferson Memorial in Washington, D.C. with the Washington Monument in the background in 1974. The helicopter was painted overall in light gray with a white cabin roof and engine/transmission fairing. (National Archives)

A Marine Corps UH-1E is escorted by a AH-1J Cobra as they fly past Makapuu Point, Oahu, in Hawaii on 10 August 1974. Both aircraft and their crews are assigned to Marine Corps Headquarters and Maintenance Squadron 24. The UH-1E is fitted with a particle separator filter over the engine air intake. (National Museum of Naval Aviation)

Infantrymen advance after exiting two UH-1H helicopters during a field training exercise in April of 1975. The insignia of the 1st Air Cavalry Division is on the Huey's nose. A low-visibility black recognition star with a tan thunderbolt across it is on the door. (DVIC)

After it delivered a load of construction supplies for a new school, a UH-1N Twin Huey takes off from the village of Amubri in Costa Rica on 4 May 1975. The construction project was part of a U.S. Air Force civic-action program. (National Archives)

At Bratsi in Costa Rica a UH-1N from the U.S. Air Force's 24th Composite Group takes off with a cargo of construction supplies for new schools that USAF personnel built as a civic-action project in outlying villages on 24 May 1975. (National Archives)

A ground crewman guides the pilot of a U.S. Air Force UH-1N Twin Huey as he prepares to land at Hill Air Force Base in Utah in 1975. No. 649 is painted in white on the nose. The Huey wears the Southeast Asia camouflage scheme, which includes tan, green, and dark green over light gray. (National Archives)

During the U.S. Bicentennial year of 1976, the armed services painted several aircraft in special commemorative markings. A short-fuselage UH-1P has diagonal red, white, and blue stripes on the tail boom with the U.S. Bicentennial logo superimposed over the white band. (National Archives)

JUH-1 SOTAS (Stand-Off Target Acquisition System) parks in the Republic of Korea in May 1976. The JUH-1 SOTAS featured the AN/APS-94 radar system in a rotating boom on the belly. The landing skids retracted in flight to allow clearance for the radar to rotate. (National Archives)

This JUH-1 SOTAS technology demonstrator was in Korea in May 1976. It featured an autopilot system and upgraded navigational avionics. The AN/APS-94 radar was connected by datalink to a ground station for analysis of the radar images. A smiley face was painted onto the end of this particular rotating boom. (National Archives)

UH-1N Twin Huey 158764, based at Naval Air Station Corpus Christi in Texas, displays U.S. Bicentennial markings in July 1976 near downtown Corpus Christi. Additionally, a Texas state flag was emblazoned on the engine fairing. (National Museum of Naval Aviation)

A UH-1N Twin Huey has No. 04 painted on the nose and U.S. Bicentennial markings in January of 1977. The Department of Defense maintained 10 UH-1N Twin Hueys for special missions at Andrews Air Force Base in Maryland. (National Archives)

UH-1N Twin Huey 158259 assigned to Search and Rescue at Marine Corps Air Station Yuma in Arizona parks on a pad on 16 June 1977. The tail skid has yellow and red candy stripes. (National Museum of Naval Aviation)

An Army UH-1H helicopter with simulated casualties aboard arrives at an air-transportable field hospital during Exercise Wounded Eagle '82 at Fort Irwin, California. On the sliding door is a red cross with a white No. 247 superimposed on it. (DVIC)

Members of the 2nd Medical Battalion load a "casualty" aboard a UH-1H ambulance helicopter for medevac during the joint South Korea / U.S. Exercise Team Spirit '84 in March of 1984. "DUSTOFF" and "088" are stenciled in white on the sliding door. (DVIC)

An OPFOR (Opposing Forces) Aviation Hind, a visually-modified (vismod) UH-1H, hovers over the helipad near the 32nd Guards Motorized Rifle Regiment at the National Training Center (NTC) at Fort Irwin in 1986. Multiple Integrated Laser Engagement System (MILES) transmitters on the stubs send kill information to BluFor air and ground targets. A yellow kill-indicator light is located on the starboard skid. (U.S. Army)

OPFOR Aviation 10 is parked at the Bicycle Lake Army Airfield inside the NTC in 1986. The UH-1H is a vismod of an armored Soviet Mi-24E Hind attack helicopter. (U.S. Army)

OPFOR Aviation 01, a vismod UH-1H, banks near Three Corners during a force-on-force rotation at the National Training Center in Fort Irwin, California, in the spring of 1989. Vismod Hueys were the aggressor threat at the NTC from 1985 until 2011. (Paul Hamblin)

Cpl. Geoff Cottrell of A Company, 6th Battalion, 31st Infantry, prepares for an OPFOR attack run at the NTC in 1986. The OPFOR platoon of the NTC Aviation Company has an Army-wide reputation for excellence in aggressive tactics and individual pilot skills that results in the world's most realistic force-on-force training. (Geoff Cottrell collection)

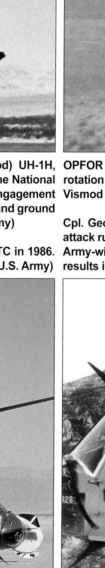

A West German Luftwaffe UH-1H, side No. 71+32, flies during an Autobahn landing exercise near the city of Ahlhorn in 1985. The Federal Republic of Germany was one of the foreign users of UH-1s. A shield-type insignia is on the auxiliary door. (DVIC)

A recovery crew uses the crane on the rear of an M816 5-ton wrecker to hoist a damaged UH-1 helicopter onto a flatbed trailer at New Boston in New Hampshire in December 1989. The tail rotor drive shaft is exposed and stretches down the tail boom. (DVIC)

A UH-1H helicopter of Battery B, 1st Battalion, 159th Aviation Regiment, 18th Aviation Brigade, flies over an abandoned settlement in Saudi Arabia during Operation Desert Shield in December 1990 prior to the liberation of Kuwait. (DVIC)

A Royal Thai Army UH-1H in Southeast Asia or equivalent camouflage lifts off after it delivered a group of Thai infantrymen to a landing zone during the joint Thai-U.S. training exercise Cobra Gold '92 staged out of Korat Royal Thai Air Force Base. (DVIC)

Members of the 90th Communications Squadron Strategic Communications Maintenance Shop board a UH-1N Twin Huey from the 37th Rescue Squadron for the trip to a remote missile alert facility at F.E. Warren Air Force Base in Wyoming in October 1996. (DVIC)

Members of Marine Wing Support Squadron 271 (MWSS-271) recover a downed Marine Corps UH-1N Twin Huey helicopter a short distance north of Baghdad in support of Operation Iraqi Freedom in April 2003. Damage appears to be fairly light. (DVIC)

A UH-1Y Venom of Marine Medium Helicopter Squadron (HMM) 163 (Reinforced) (HMM-163), 13th Marine Expeditionary Unit, prepares to land on a ship on 3 June 2003. The low-visibility markings include a faint No. 39 on the sliding door. (DVIDS)

Two U.S. Army UH-1H Huey helicopters from the Colorado Army National Guard make their final flight on 12 December 2004 from Buckley Air Force Base in Colorado. These Hueys were headed to Temple, Texas, where they would be retired from service. (DVIC)

79

Marines aboard a UH-1Y Venom survey a trail on Camp Pendleton on 22 July 2016. While all UH-1 variants were retired from active U.S. Army service in 2005, the Marines' UH-1Y was upgraded for 21st century combat and will carry on the heritage of active-service Hueys into the foreseeable future. (Lance Cpl. Samuel D. Brusseau / USMC)